Copyright © 2025 by Highlights for Children

All rights reserved. Copying or digitizing this book for storage, display, or distribution in any other medium is strictly prohibited.

For information about permission to reprint selections from this book, please contact permissions@highlights.com.

Published by Highlights Press
815 Church Street
Honesdale, Pennsylvania 18431

ISBN: 978-1-63962-383-9
Library of Congress Control Number: 2025932721
Manufactured In: Heshan, Guangdong, China
Mfg. 06/2025
Visit Highlights.com.
10 9 8 7 6 5 4 3 2 1

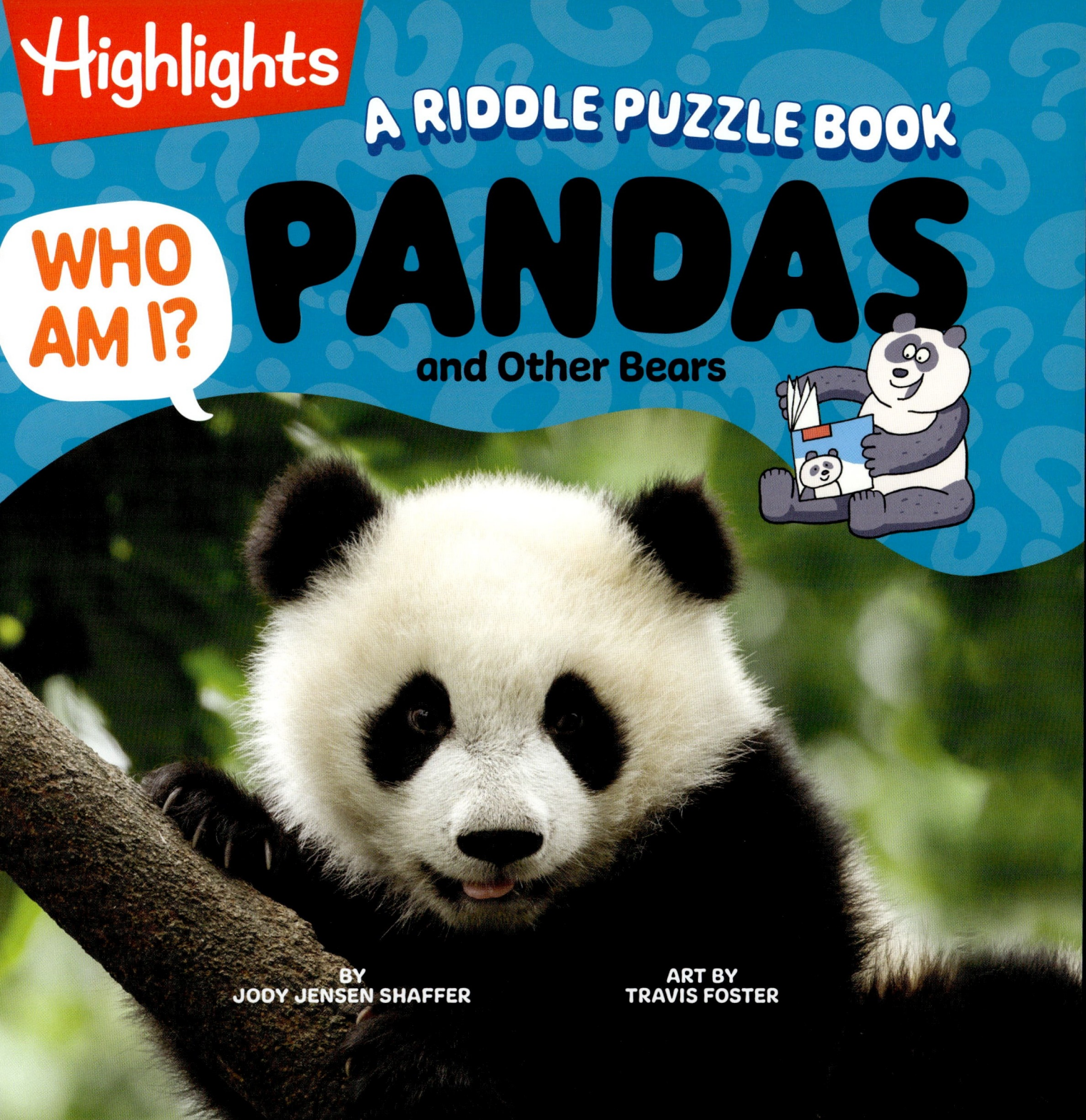

I lumber around. I tumble with ease.
My black-and-white fur blends into the trees.
The mountains are misty. My den is warm,
and that's where my tiny babies are born.

Bamboo is my favorite. I munch and I munch.
My strong jaws help me bite down and crunch.
But eating a lot makes me slump in a heap.
After meals, I curl up and fall right to sleep.

WHO AM I?

I am a GIANT PANDA!

I have wristbones that act like **THUMBS.**

Bamboo makes up **99%** of my diet.

I can eat **DOZENS OF POUNDS** of bamboo in one day!

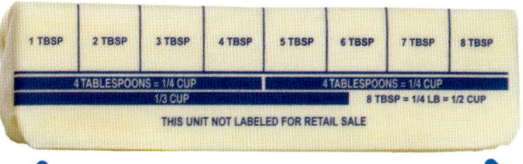

I'm about the size of a **STICK OF BUTTER** when I'm born.

I spend **10 to 16 HOURS** a day eating.

Time to eat again!

My bite strength is similar to a **LION'S.**

I'm small, but I'm strong.
I climb up tall trees.
I sleep on platforms
made of branches and leaves.

My tongue licks up bugs.
Termites are the best.
A patch of gold fur sits
on my neck and chest.

WHO AM I?

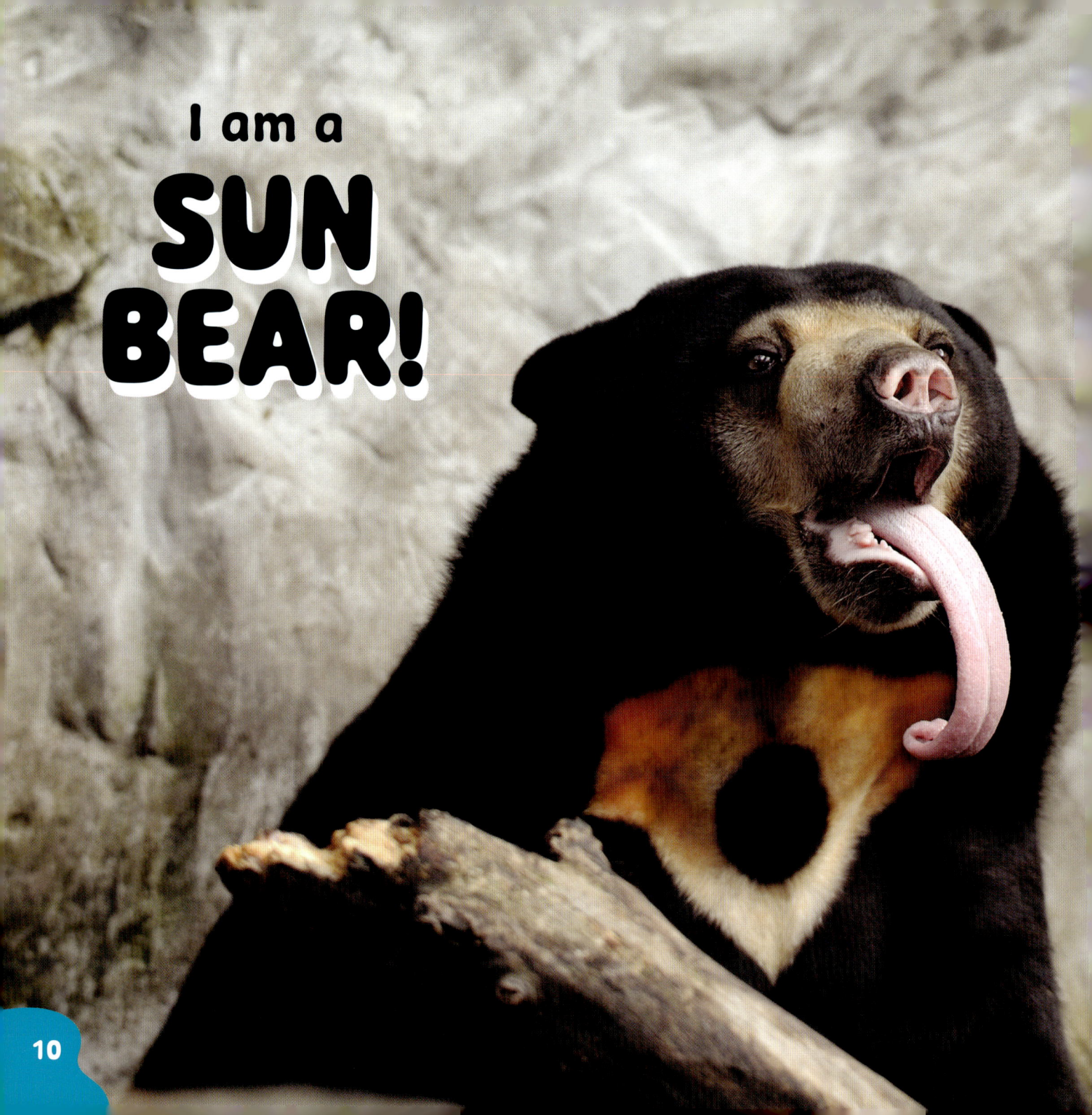

I am a SUN BEAR!

I don't **HIBERNATE** in winter.

Hibernation? Thanks, but no thanks!

I have **4-INCH-LONG CURVED CLAWS** for digging and climbing.

I use my **10-INCH-LONG TONGUE** to slurp up termites and honey.

I AM THE smallest OF ALL THE BEAR SPECIES.

When I'm feeling friendly, I make a **CLUCKING NOISE** like a hen.

Cluck, cluck, I'm your friend.

I sometimes **STAND UPRIGHT** while cradling my cubs.

Despite the name I go by,
I'm neither sluggish nor slow.
I bound through hot, dry grasslands
and cool off where rivers flow.

My shaggy fur keeps me safe
from biting bugs and heat.
I carry babies on my back,
and I search for ants to eat.

WHO AM I?

I am a
SLOTH BEAR!

I'm the only bear that carries my cubs around **ON MY BACK.**

Thanks for the lift, Mom!

I LOUDLY SLURP insects through a gap in my teeth.

I can **SEAL UP MY NOSTRILS** while eating so bugs don't get in.

I eat **TENS OF THOUSANDS OF INSECTS** a day.

MENU
APPETIZERS: BUGS
MAIN COURSE: BUGS
DESSERT: BUGS

I can smell termites that are **3 FEET** underground.

Do you feel a breeze?

My coat looks white, just like the snow.
I move a lot. I'm on the go!
I can weigh over a thousand pounds,
and seals scram when I make the rounds.

I take dips in the cold Arctic Sea,
my oar-like paws propelling me.
I build a den. Twin cubs arrive.
Soon, I teach them how to survive.

WHO AM I?

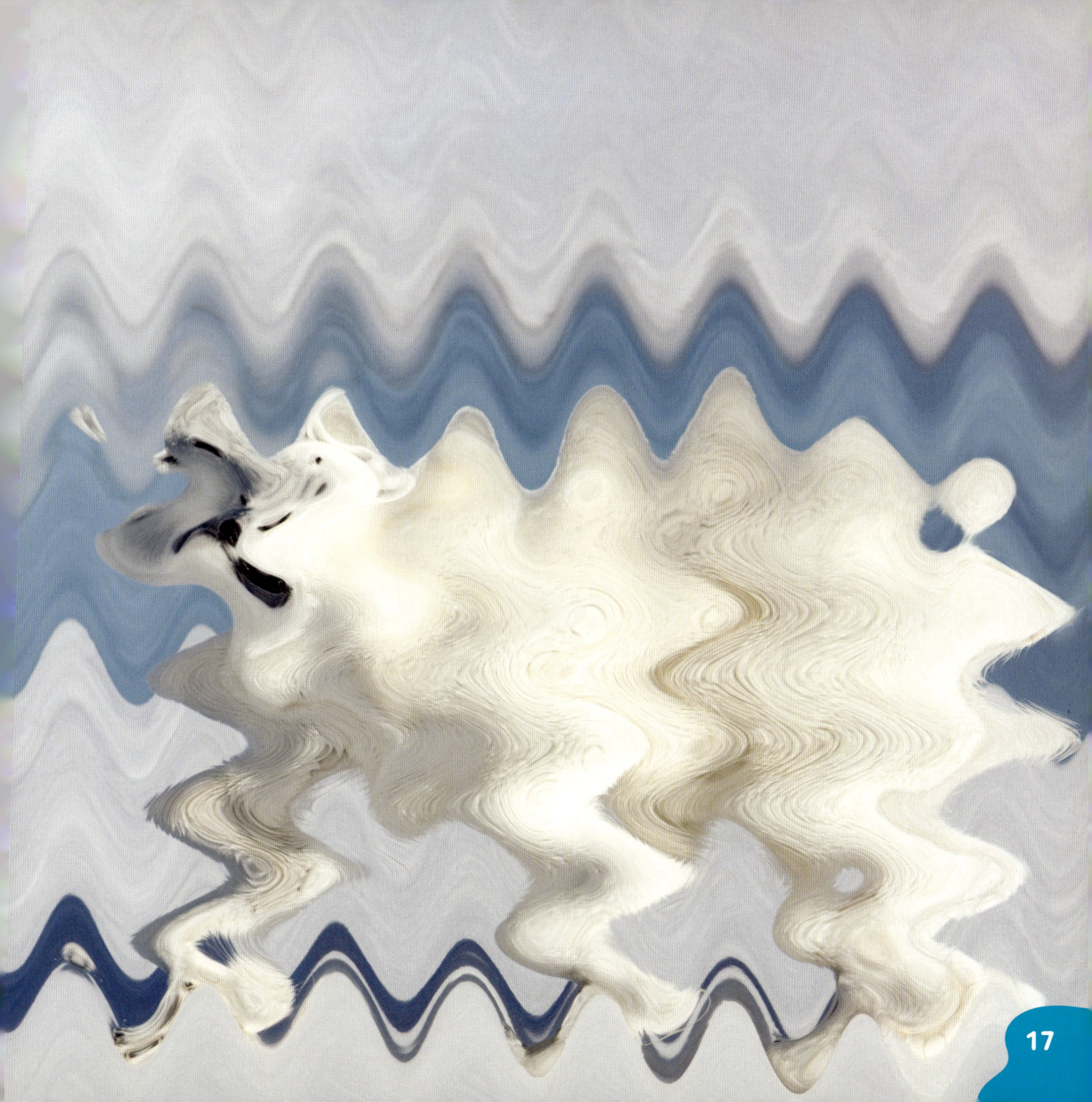

I am a
POLAR BEAR!

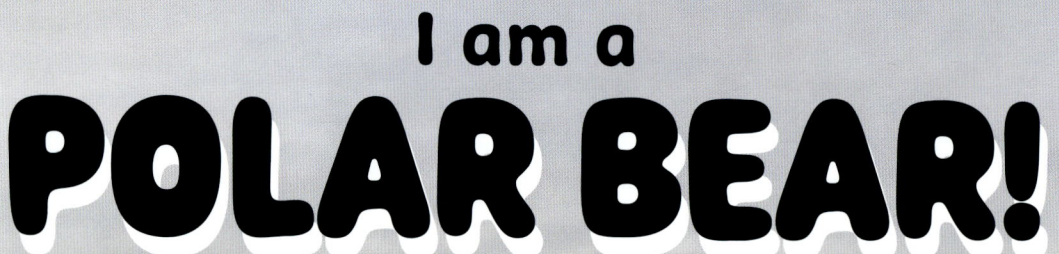

 **MY PAWS** can be almost the same width as professional baseball gloves.

I can stand **10 FEET TALL** on my hind legs.

I may **SWIM LONG DISTANCES** for hours at a time.

My cubs grow **20 TIMES** their original body weight in their first few months.

 I'm a growing cub!

I'm the only bear species considered a **MARINE ANIMAL.**

I have **FUR** at the bottom of my paws for additional warmth.

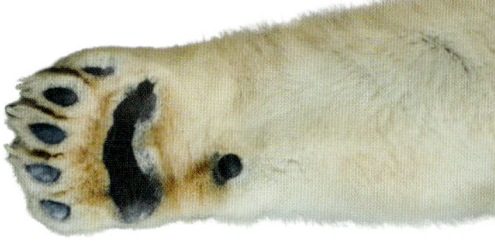

19

I have long claws to dig for food,
plus a hump upon my back.
My favorite dish is salmon fish,
with berries for a snack.

In warmer months, I eat and eat
to bulk up on my weight.
I spend the winter in my den
from five months up to eight.

WHO AM I?

The muscular **HUMP ON MY BACK** gives me extra strength for digging.

I can **RUN 30 MILES** an hour.

I am a type of **BROWN BEAR.**

Many grizzlies love eating **GLACIER LILIES.**

My name comes from the word **GRIZZLED,** which describes my silver-tipped fur.

During hibernation, my heart rate can drop as low as **5 BEATS PER MINUTE.**

My claws are curved for climbing trees
and marking where I've been.
I like to use the trails I know.
I winter in a den.

I travel long distances
and then return each night.
My sense of smell is excellent,
much better than my sight.

WHO AM I?

I am an AMERICAN BLACK BEAR!

I eat
ANTS, BEES, PINE CONES, and more.

I can pick up a scent from **OVER A MILE AWAY.**

I can climb **100 FEET** of a tree in just **30 SECONDS.**

My cubs make a **PURRING SOUND** when relaxed.

I'm the **MOST COMMON BEAR** found in North America.

Nearly **1 MILLION** of us black bears live on this continent.

27

MORE MYSTERY BEARS!

Can you guess who these other bears are?

1 I'm a species of bear from South America. Some people say the markings on my face look like a big pair of glasses!

2 I'm a species of bear often found in the hills and mountains of Asia. Sometimes I'm called the moon bear because of the moon-like marking on my chest.

3 Surprise—my fur may be white or cream colored, but I'm actually a type of American black bear!

4 I'm a type of brown bear that lives in Asia's Gobi Desert.

5 I'm a type of brown bear found only on Kodiak Island and other nearby islands off the coast of Alaska.

Answers: 1. spectacled (or Andean) bear, 2. Asiatic black bear, 3. spirit bear, 4. Gobi bear, 5. Kodiak bear.

QUIZ TIME!

1. Bamboo makes up how much of a panda's diet?

    a. 1%
    b. 50%
    c. 80%
    d. 99%

2. True or False? The sun bear is the smallest bear species.

3. What does a sloth bear do to prevent insects from crawling up its nose?

    a. It yells "Boo!" to scare them away.
    b. It seals up its nostrils.
    c. It covers its nose with its paw.
    d. Nothing. It lets the bugs crawl inside.

Put your bear knowledge to the test.

4. Why does a polar bear have fur on the bottom of its paws?

    a. To help keep the paws warm.
    b. To protect its claws.
    c. To help the bear swim faster.
    d. To sweep dirt from the ground.

5. How low can a grizzly bear's heart rate drop when hibernating?

    a. 1 beat every three minutes.
    b. 5 beats per minute.
    c. 50 beats per minute.
    d. 95 beats per minute.

6. What is the most common species of bear in North America?

    a. The sun bear.
    b. The sloth bear.
    c. The brown bear.
    d. The American black bear.

Answers: 1. d, 2. true, 3. b, 4. a, 5. b, 6. d

31

GLOSSARY

GRIZZLED: Streaked or sprinkled with gray hair

HIBERNATE: To pass the winter in a sleeping or resting state

MARINE: Relating to the sea

MUSCULAR: Having strong muscles

SPECIES: A group of living things that have a common ancestor

YOU'LL ALSO LIKE:

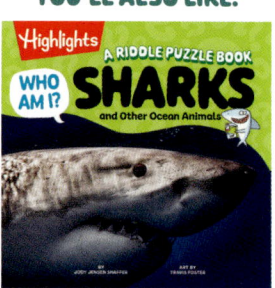

All Getty Images, except: 11, 15, 23, 28: Alamy (claws, sniffing sloth bear, glacier lily, Andean/spectacled bear); 29: Hunter J. Causey, Wikimedia (Gobi bear).